THE
Vintage Flower
SAMPLER QUILT

ABOUT THE AUTHOR

Atsuko Matsuyama is one of Japan's leading quilt artists and fabric designers. In 1989, she opened her quilt studio A-Two. She often exhibits her work at leading quilt festivals in Japan and teaches workshops around the world. Her work is regularly featured in quilting publications and she is the author of several books, including *Happy Flower Quilts* and *Sew Cute Quilts and Gifts*. Matsuyama also designs fabrics for Yuwa, Japan. Follow her on Instagram @quiltstudioa_two.

The Vintage Flower Sampler Quilt
Published in 2023 by Zakka Workshop, a division of
World Book Media LLC

www.zakkaworkshop.com
134 Federal Street
Salem, MA 01970 USA
info@zakkaworkshop.com

Editors: Lindsay Fair & Kristyne Czepuryk
Technical writer: Kristyne Czepuryk
Illustrator: Kristyne Czepuryk
Photography: Glenn Scott
Top and bottom photos on page 8 and all fabric photos on page 9 by Kristyne Czepuryk
Middle photo on page 8 by Rita Hodge

Props provided by Vintage on 2
Translator: Kyoko Matthews
Production: Christy Bao
Publisher: Genia Patestides

ISBN: 978-1-940552-74-3

Printed in China
10 9 8 7 6 5 4 3 2

THE
Vintage Flower
SAMPLER QUILT

A Step-By-Step Guide To Sewing
A Stunning Quilt & Fresh Projects

ATSUKO MATSUYAMA

Contents

FOREWORD

I've been a crafter all my life, a quilter for almost 40 years, a pattern designer, published author, and occasional fabric designer. My personal aesthetic can be summed up in three words: pink, bows, and lace. When I first discovered the work of Atsuko Matsuyama, it was like finding a kindred spirit. The details in her work are very much in keeping with everything I love about Japanese quilting, with one significant difference: she works with bright, cheerful feedsack reproduction fabrics, many of which she designs herself.

Atsuko's gentle interpretations of vintage feedsack prints are the centerpiece of her very pretty aesthetic that is filled with fanciful images of florals, delicious fruits, ribbons, bows, and lace. Then she applies a fresh color palette that features bright, candy-colored hues, starting with her favorite color, pink—a bond we share! But she doesn't stop there. She seamlessly mixes both patchwork and appliqué, and loves to embellish her quilts and projects with little hints of embroidery to enhance the look and feel of her work. The majority of her quilts are sewn by hand, making them true works of art.

Happy Flower Quilts, Atsuko's first book published in English, was released in 2016. Packed with adorable projects, the star of the book was a gorgeous sampler quilt composed of 99 unique blocks. Like me, so many quilters instantly fell in love with this quilt and set out to make their own versions.

Inspired by the warm reception of *Happy Flower Quilts*, Atsuko has created a fresh new sampler in her signature style that was designed specifically to make it more accessible to quilters. *The Vintage Flower Sampler Quilt* is chockfull of photos showcasing all the special details of the quilt and projects, as well as step-by-step diagrams for constructing each block from start to finish. The sampler itself is composed of larger 12" blocks that are more machine-sewing friendly for those that prefer to sew by machine rather than by hand. Anyone who has ever puzzled their way through a Japanese quilting book will be thrilled to see the user-friendly features of this book— everything is designed in inches, seam allowance is included in all templates, and there are even tips and tricks for sewing by machine.

So if you, dear reader, are like me and love to make pretty things with fabric, including lovely quilts to elevate your home, handmade accessories to keep your sewing space tidy or store little treasures, then you will be delighted beyond compare with the charming and useful objects Atsuko has designed for us in this book.

Kristyne Czepuryk
Pretty by Hand

SELECTING FABRICS FOR YOUR SAMPLER QUILT

One of my favorite things about quilting is combining lots of different colorful fabrics to create a scrappy, vintage look. I like to incorporate three main types of fabrics into my work to achieve this look.

Reproduction 30s Fabrics

I have been designing fabric for over 25 years. I was inspired to start designing after I was unable to find cute, colorful patchwork fabric—in those days, all the quilting fabric on the market was very dark. I draw my inspiration from vintage feedsacks, antique American postcards, and illustrations. My fabric collections are available through Yuwa Fabrics.

Vintage Feedsacks

I have been collecting vintage feedsacks for years. When I first started my collection, I purchased the fabric through an importer here in Japan. After a while, I began attending International Quilt Festival in Houston and purchased many beautiful feedsacks from vendors there. I have also purchased a few at quilt festivals in Tokyo and through American dealers. I used to buy them on eBay auctions as well, but they have become quite expensive online.

Geometric Fabrics

Some of my favorite prints including stripes, plaids, ginghams, small polka dots, and *chidori goshi*, which is the Japanese phrase for houndstooth check.

Tips on Combining Fabrics

I usually start by selecting the fabric for the largest part of the design as this will become the focus for the block. Once I've made a decision on the first fabric I plan to use, I bring that color into my next selection. I always try to mix both small and large scale prints, and incorporate many different colors and patterns. If all the patterns used have the same scale, the overall effect tends to become a bit boring.

Example block: Lost Children on page 28

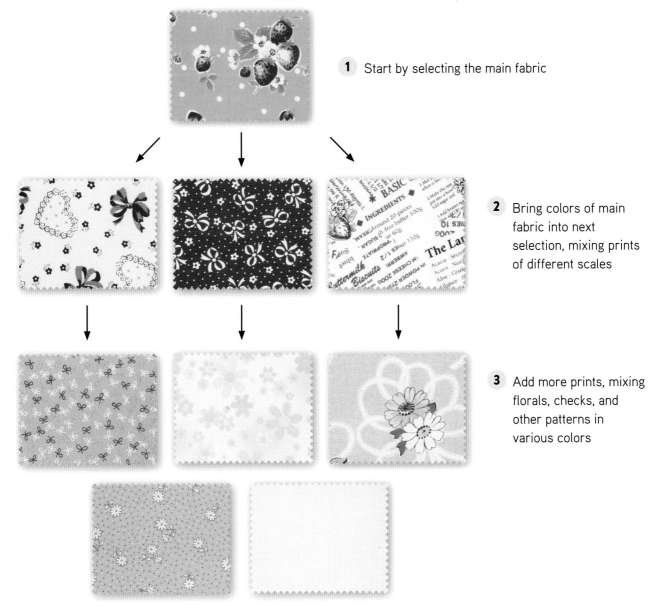

1 Start by selecting the main fabric

2 Bring colors of main fabric into next selection, mixing prints of different scales

3 Add more prints, mixing florals, checks, and other patterns in various colors

ANATOMY OF A SAMPLER BLOCK

Now that we've discussed the different types of fabric used, let's take a closer look at how to utilize these fabrics to create interesting patchwork and appliqué blocks. Included below are two blocks from the Vintage Flower Sampler Quilt: Cross Plains (see page 20) and Apples (see page 58). Let's examine these blocks and discuss how color, scale, and pattern influence the overall design.

Tip #1

If you look closely, you'll see that at least one small triangle in each motif is composed of a different color fabric. My first quilting teacher taught me this trick of introducing different colors and patterns in unexpected places to add movement to the design. This "make do with what you have" philosophy influenced designs of Depression-era quilts and has also inspired my style.

Tip #2

Use fabric with a different scale print for one motif to create movement within the block.

Tip #3

I chose a lighter color fabric for one of the four apples for a bit of contrast.

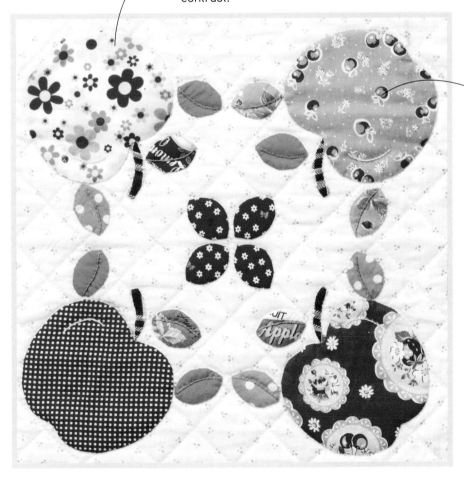

Tip #4

I like to use a print fabric that features the same motif as the appliqué design. This adds a dose of playfulness to the block.

THE
Patchwork
BLOCKS

Corn AND Beans

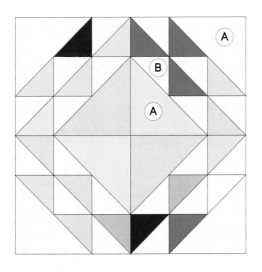

Cutting Instructions

A (4) 4⅞" squares, cut diagonally to make (8) triangles

B (20) 2⅞" squares, cut diagonally to make (40) triangles

Notes: Cutting dimensions include seam allowance. Sew all blocks with ¼" seam allowance. The center A triangles are pressed in opposite directions.

1 Sew (10) **B** together. Make 4.

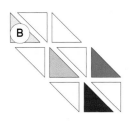 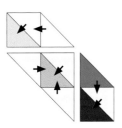 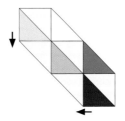

Make 4

2 Add (2) **A**. Make (4) pieced squares.

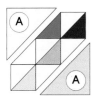 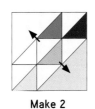

Make 2   Make 2

3 Join the pieced squares.

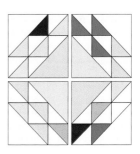

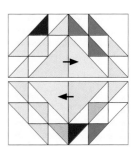

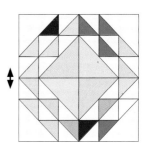

Cat's CRADLE

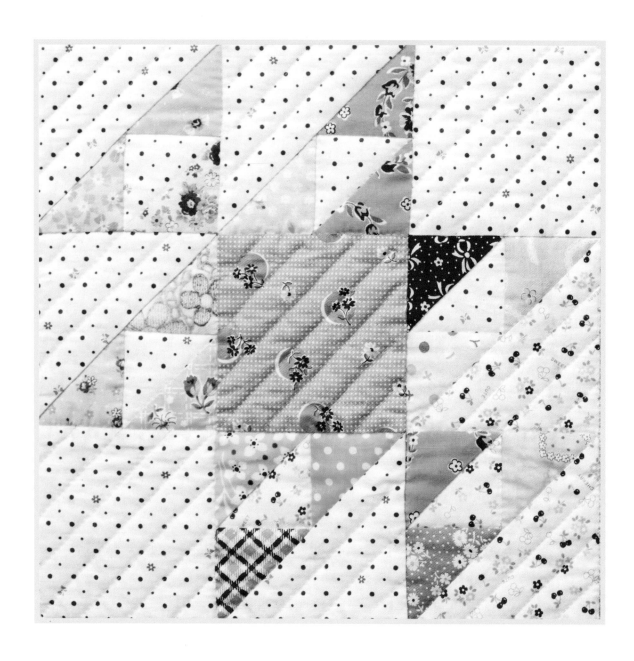

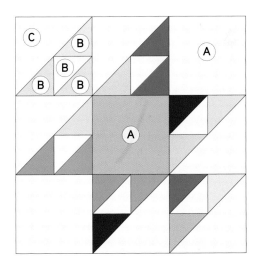

Cutting Instructions

A (3) 4½" squares
B (12) 2⅞" squares, cut diagonally
to make (24) triangles
C (3) 4⅞" squares, cut diagonally
to make (6) triangles

Notes: Cutting dimensions include seam allowance. Sew all blocks with ¼" seam allowance.

1 Sew (4) **B** together. Make 6.

Make 6

2 Add **C**. Make 6 pieced squares.

Make 6

3 Join (3) **A** and the pieced squares.

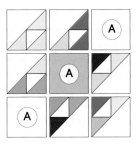 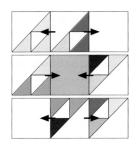

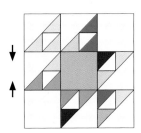

Rolling STONES

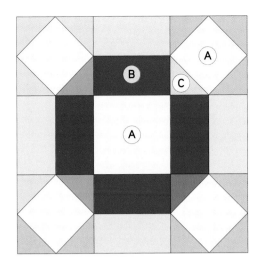

Cutting Instructions

A (5) 4½" squares
B (8) 2½" × 4½" rectangles
C (16) 2½" squares

Notes: Cutting dimensions include seam allowance. Sew all blocks with ¼" seam allowance.

1 Join 2 **B**. Make 4.

Make 4

2 Using Sew and Flip (see page 38), add (4) **C** to each **A**. Make 4.

Make 4

3 Join **A** and the pieced units.

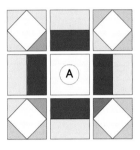

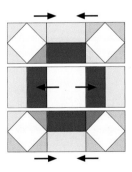

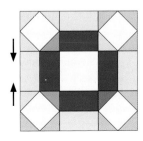

CROSS *Plains*

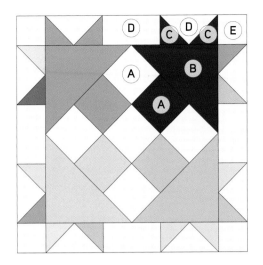

Cutting Instructions

A (9) 2⅝" squares
B (4) 5⅜" squares, cut diagonally to make 8 triangles (need 4)
C (16) 2" squares
D (12) 2" × 3½" rectangles
E (4) 2" squares

Notes: Cutting dimensions include seam allowance. Sew all blocks with ¼" seam allowance. Ensure the adjacent A/B pieces are of matching fabrics to create the desired effect.

---

1 Sew (9) **A** together to make a nine-patch.

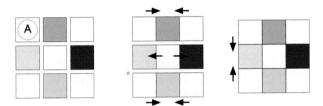

2 Add (4) **B** to the nine-patch, matching the **B** fabric to the adjacent **A** fabric.

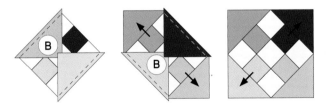

3 Using Sew and Flip (see page 38), add (2) **C** to **D** to make a flying geese unit. Make 8.

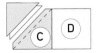 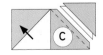

Make 8

4 Join (2) flying geese to **D** to make a side border. Make 2.

Make 2

5 Join (2) flying geese, **D**, and (2) **E** to make a top border. Make a bottom border.

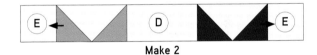

Make 2

6 Join the side borders and then the top/bottom borders.

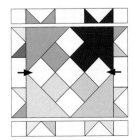 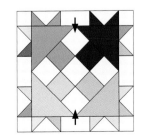

Pineapple

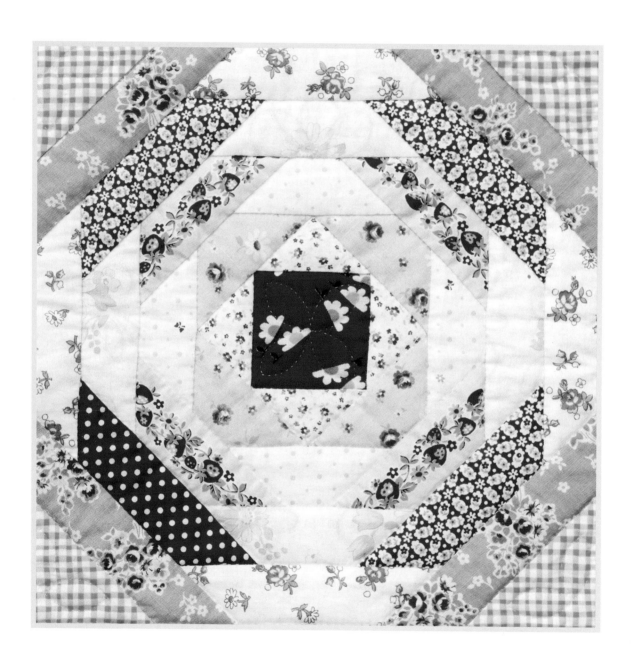

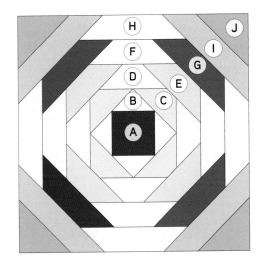

Cutting Instructions

A (1) 2¾" square
B (2) 2½" squares, cut diagonally to make (4) triangles
C (4) from template
D (4) from template
E (4) from template

F (4) from template
G (4) from template
H (4) from template
I (4) from template
J (2) 3⅝" squares, cut diagonally to make (4) triangles

Notes: Cutting dimensions include seam allowance. Sew all blocks with ¼" seam allowance. Test seam allowances first to ensure accuracy. See pages 105-106 for templates. Press all seams outward.

1 Add (4) **B** to **A**.

2 Add (4) **C**.

3 Continue to add the **D**, **E**, **F**, **G**, **H**, and **I** rings.

  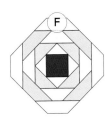  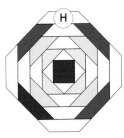 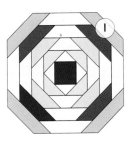

4 Add (4) **J**. The **J** triangles are a bit larger than required. Trim the block to 12½" × 12½".

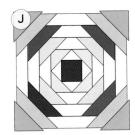 

Around THE WORLD

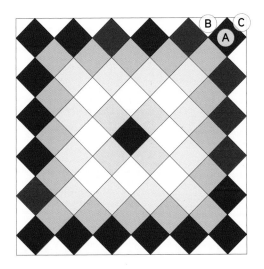

Cutting Instructions

A (61) from template (21 red, 16 pink, 12 yellow, 8 light blue, and 4 aqua)

B (5) 3¾" squares, cut twice to make (20) triangles

C (2) 2¼" squares, cut once to make (4) triangles

Notes: Cutting dimensions include seam allowance. Sew all blocks with ¼" seam allowance. See page 108 for template. **B** and **C** are cut larger than required for trimming. Press all seams open.

1   Join the (61) **A** squares into 9 rows.

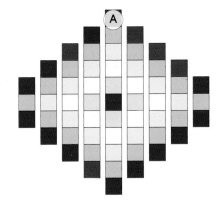

2   Add (2) **B** to the ends of each row, except the middle row.

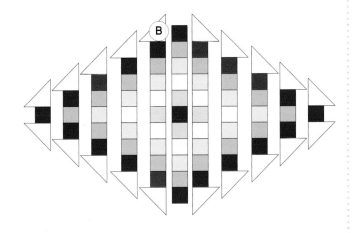

3   Join the rows. Then add the (4) **C**.

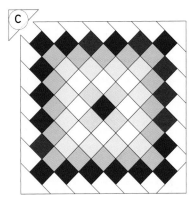

4   Trim the block to 12½" × 12½", leaving a ¼" seam allowance.

Parisienne

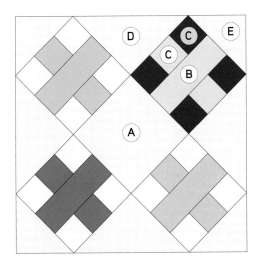

Cutting Instructions

A (1) from template
B (4) from template
C (24) from template
D (4) from template
E (2) 4" squares, cut diagonally to make (4) triangles

Notes: Cutting dimensions include seam allowance.
Sew all blocks with ¼" seam allowance. See pages 107-108 for templates.

1 Join (6) **C** and (1) **B**. Make 4.

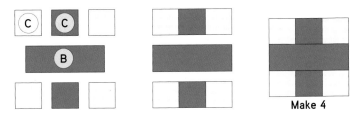

Make 4

2 Join **A**, (4) **D**, and the pieced squares.

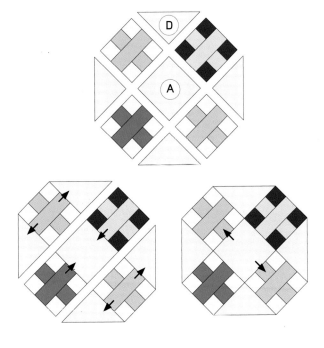

3 Add (4) **E**. The E triangles are a bit larger than required. Trim the block to 12½" × 12½".

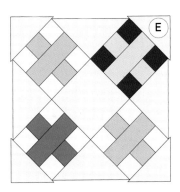

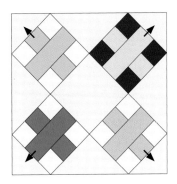

Lost CHILDREN

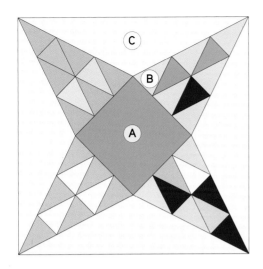

Cutting Instructions

A (1) 4¾" square
B (36) from template
C (4) from template

Notes: Cutting dimensions include seam allowance. Sew all blocks with ¼" seam allowance. See page 109 for templates.

1 Sew (9) **B** together to make a star point. Make 4.

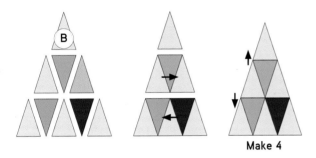

Make 4

2 Add 2 star points to opposite sides of **A**, leaving the ¼" seam allowances unstitched.

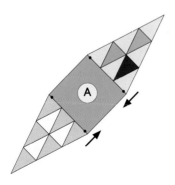

3 Add 2 **C** to a star point, leaving the ¼" seam allowances unstitched. Make 2.

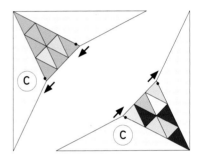

4 Using inset seams (see page 38), join the 3 pieced sections.

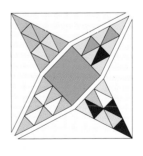 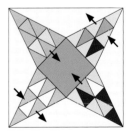

Farmer's DAUGHTER

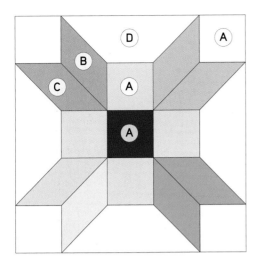

Cutting Instructions

A (9) from template
B (4) from template
C (4) from template
D (4) from template

Notes: Cutting dimensions include seam allowance. Sew all blocks with ¼" seam allowance. See pages 110-111 for templates.

1 Using an inset seam (see page 38), join **B** and **C**, leaving the ¼" seam allowance that will meet **A** unstitched. Then add **A**. Make 4.

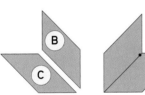 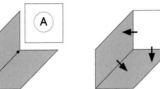

Make 4

2 Join (5) **A** and the inset corners, leaving the ¼" seam allowances that will meet **D** in the next step unstitched.

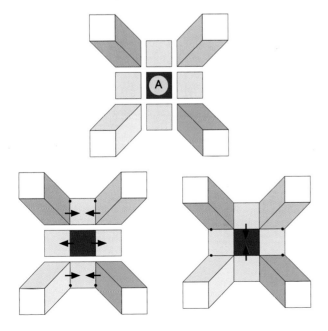

3 Using inset seams, add (4) **D**.

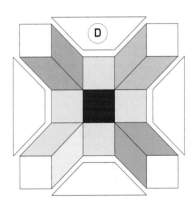

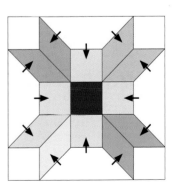

Tallahassee

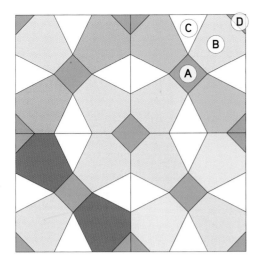

Cutting Instructions

A (5) from template
B (16) from template
C (16) from template
D (6) 2" squares, cut diagonally to make (12) triangles

Notes: Cutting dimensions include seam allowance. Sew all blocks with ¼" seam allowance. See page 112 for templates. Pay attention to which corners will be joined to the center **A**.

1 Join (2) **B** to **A**, leaving the ¼" seam allowance unstitched.

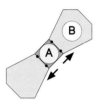

2 Join (2) **C** to **B**, leaving the ¼" seam allowance unstitched. Make 2.

Make 2

3 Using inset seams (see page 38), join the 3 sections together. Add (3) **D**. The **D** triangles are a bit larger than required. Trim the pieced square to 6½" × 6½". Make 4.

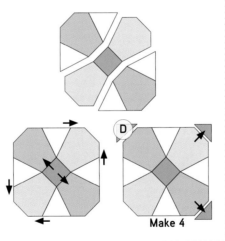

Make 4

4 Join 2 sections to **A** leaving the ¼" seam allowance unstitched.

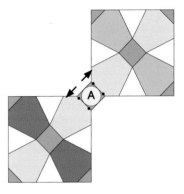

5 Using inset seams, join the 3 sections.

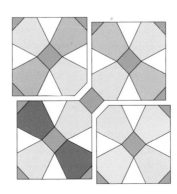
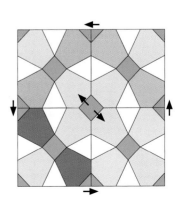

Lattice FAN

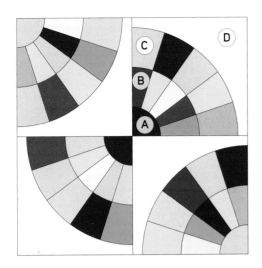

Cutting Instructions

A (4) from template
B (20) from template
C (20) from template
D (4) from template

Notes: Cutting dimensions include seam allowance. Sew all blocks with ¼" seam allowance. See page 113 for templates. Curved seams are required (see page 39).

1 Sew (5) **B** together.

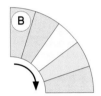

2 Sew (5) **C** together.

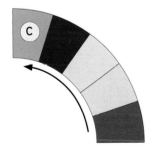

3 Join **A**, **B** arc, and **C** arc.

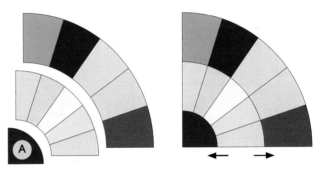

4 Add **D**. Make 4.

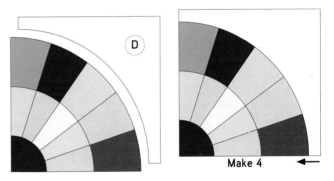

Make 4

5 Join them.

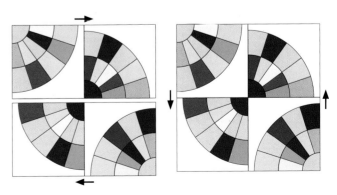

Sugar PLUM

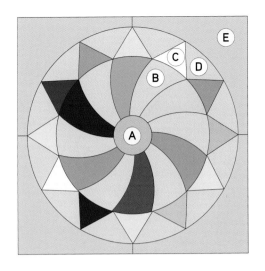

Cutting Instructions

A (1) from template   **D** (12) from template
B (12) from template   **E** (4) from template
C (12) from template

Notes: Cutting dimensions include seam allowance. Sew all blocks with ¼" seam allowance. See pages 114–115 for templates. Curved seams and appliqué are required (see pages 39 and 66).

1 Sew (12) **B** together.

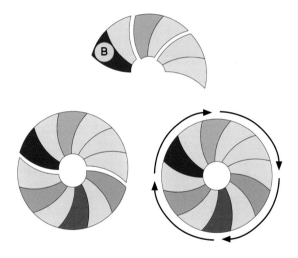

2 Sew (12) **C** and (12) **D** together.

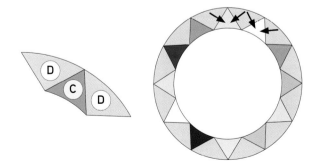

3 Appliqué the circle onto the ring (see page 66). Then appliqué **A** to the center.

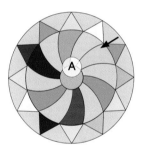

4 Join (4) **E**. Appliqué the pieced circle onto the **E** sections.

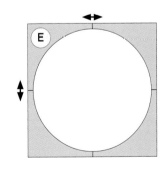
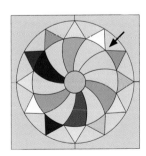

PATCHWORK TECHNIQUES

In Japan, hand sewing is very popular among patchwork quilters. Many quilters find the process of stitching by hand very relaxing. The blocks in this book can be sewn either by hand or on the machine—please choose whichever method works best for you. Whether stitching by hand or machine, here are some helpful tips and tricks to achieve beautiful results.

Sew and Flip

1 Draw or press a diagonal line on the wrong side of the top fabric.

2 Place the top square onto the bottom square, right sides together, aligning the edges. Sew on the diagonal line.

3 Trim away the excess fabric, leaving a ¼" seam allowance.

4 Fold the top square over. Press as indicated in the instructions.

Inset ("Y") Seams

1 On the wrong side of each piece, mark the ¼" point at the corners.

2 Use a pin to align the ¼" marks right sides together. Insert the sewing machine needle into the mark. Sew forward a few stitches, backstitch to the mark, then sew forward again to the end of the seam (or another mark, as indicated by the instructions).

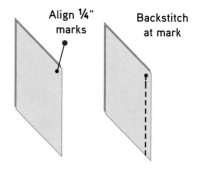

Align ¼" marks

Backstitch at mark

3 Repeat to sew one side of the third piece. Do not stitch through the seam allowance of the first seam.

4 Repeat to sew the third seam, avoiding the seam allowance.

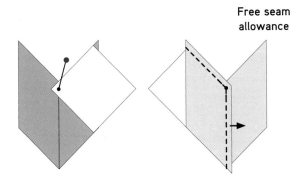

Free seam allowance

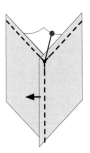

Curved Seams

1 Finger-press a fold to mark the center of each curved edge.

2 With right sides together, align and pin the centers. Then pin the outside edges.

3 Pin the remaining curve, stretching the bias edge as little as possible. Sew the pieces together.

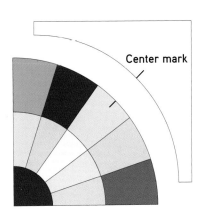

Center mark

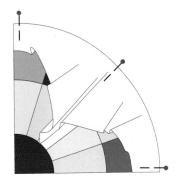

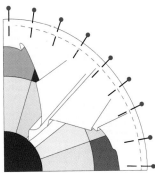

THE *Appliqué* BLOCKS

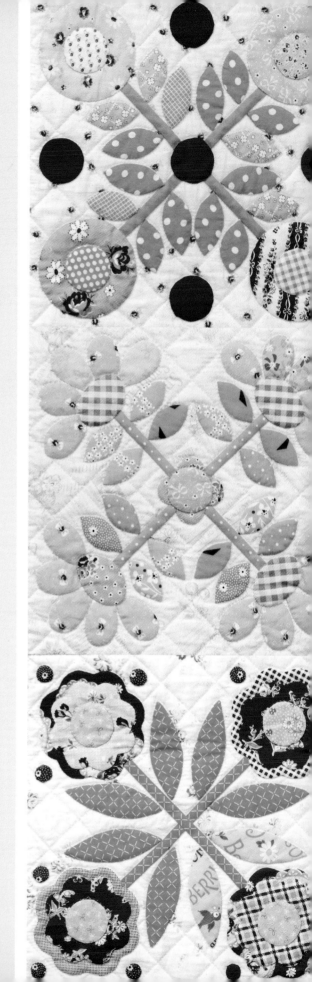

PING PONG *Mums*

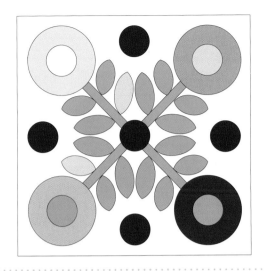

Cutting Instructions

Background fabric: (1) 13½" × 13½" square

A (2) 1" × 7¾" strips   **D** (8) from template
B (4) from template   **E** (8) from template
C (9) from template

Notes: Refer to photo on opposite page for appliqué orientation for the full block. Trim the finished block to 12½" × 12½".

FULL-SIZE TEMPLATE

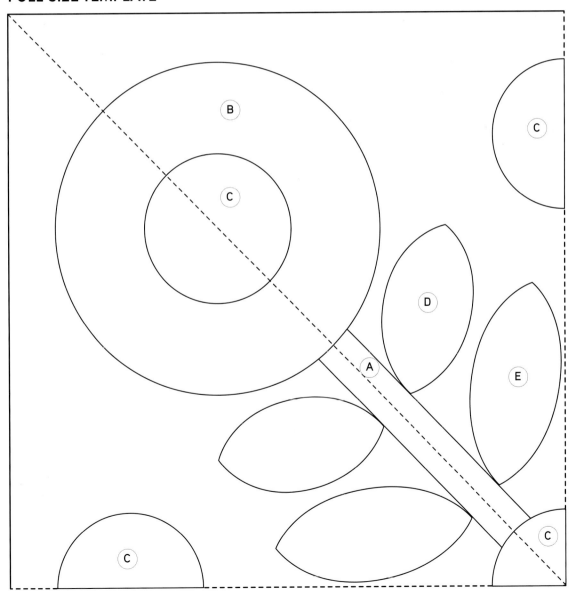

Sunflowers

Cutting Instructions

Background fabric: (1) 13½" × 13½" square

A (2) ⅞" × 8¼" strips   **C** (4) from template
B (32) from template   **D** (8) from template

Notes: Refer to photo on opposite page for appliqué orientation for the full block. Pin **C** in place before **B** to help position all the petals accurately. Stitch the **B**s, and then stitch **C**. Trim the finished block to 12½" × 12½".

FULL-SIZE TEMPLATE

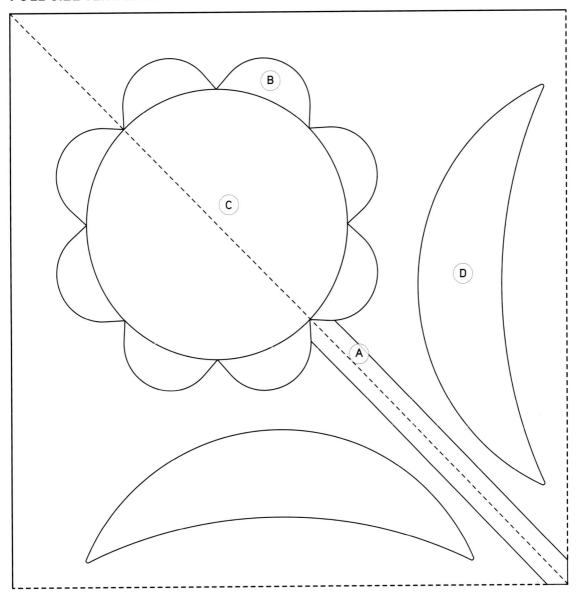

Daisy

Cutting Instructions

Background fabric: (1) 13½" × 13½" square

A (2) ⅞" × 8¼" strips
B (20) from template
C (4) from template
D (16) from template

E (4) from template
F (1) from template (use C from "Marguerite" block on page 49)

Notes: Refer to photo on opposite page for appliqué orientation for the full block. Trim the finished block to 12½" × 12½".

FULL-SIZE TEMPLATE

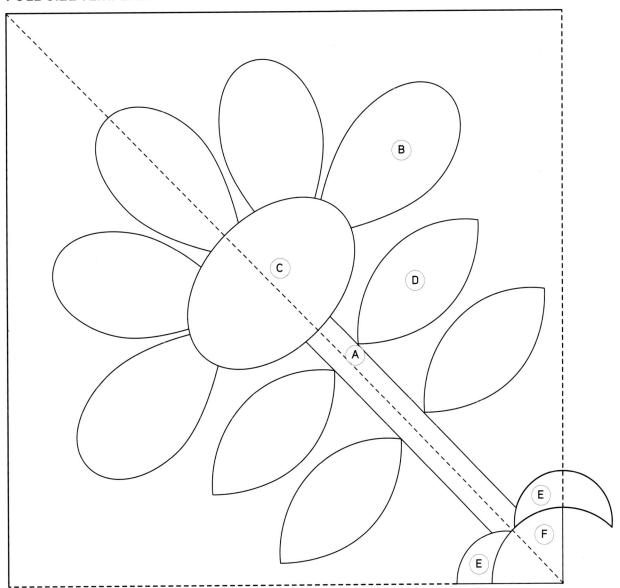

Marguerite

Cutting Instructions

Background fabric: (1) 13½" × 13½" square

A (2) ⅞" × 8¼" strips   **C** (5) from template
B (32) from template   **D** (4) from template

Notes: Refer to photo on opposite page for appliqué orientation for the full block. Trim the finished block to 12½" × 12½".

FULL-SIZE TEMPLATE

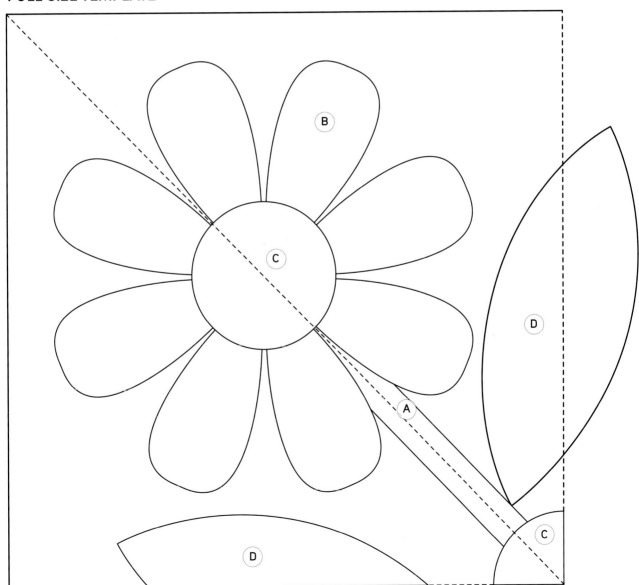

Tulips

Cutting Instructions

Background fabric: (1) 13½" × 13½" square

A (2) 1" × 7¾" strips   **D** (4) from template
B (8) from template   **E** (8) from template
C (4) from template   **F** (16) from template

Notes: Refer to photo on opposite page for appliqué orientation for the full block. Trim the finished block to 12½" × 12½".

FULL-SIZE TEMPLATE

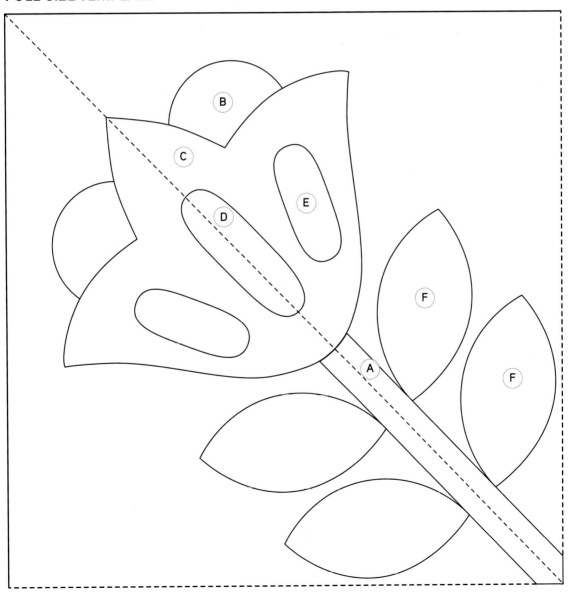

Rose

Cutting Instructions

Background fabric (1) 13½" × 13½" square

A (2) 1" × 6¾" strips
B (4) from template
C (4) from template

D (4) from template
E (8) from template
F (12) from template

Notes: Refer to photo on opposite page for appliqué orientation for the full block. Trim the finished block to 12½" × 12½".

FULL-SIZE TEMPLATE

Grapes

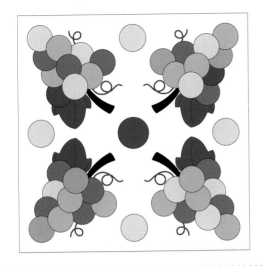

Cutting Instructions

Background fabric: (1) 13½" × 13½" square

A (4) from template
B (44) from template
C (4) from template

D (1) from template (use C from "Marguerite" block on page 49)

Notes: Refer to photo on opposite page for appliqué orientation for the full block. Embroider the colored lines with stem stitch using 3 plies of floss (see page 67). Trim the finished block to 12½" × 12½".

FULL-SIZE TEMPLATE

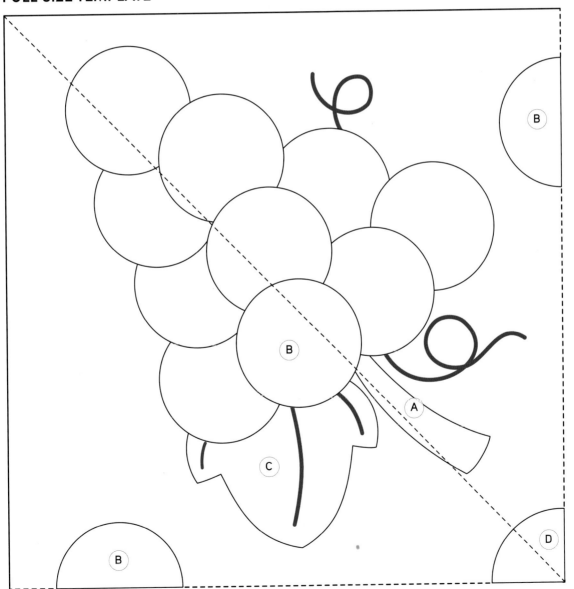

Oranges

Cutting Instructions

Background fabric: (1) 13½" × 13½" square

A (8) from template   **D** (40) from template
B (8) from template   **E** (4) from template
C (4) from template   **F** (4) from template

Notes: Refer to photo on opposite page for appliqué orientation for the full block. Embroider the colored lines with stem stitch using 3 plies of floss (see page 67). Trim the finished block to 12½" × 12½".

FULL-SIZE TEMPLATE

Apples

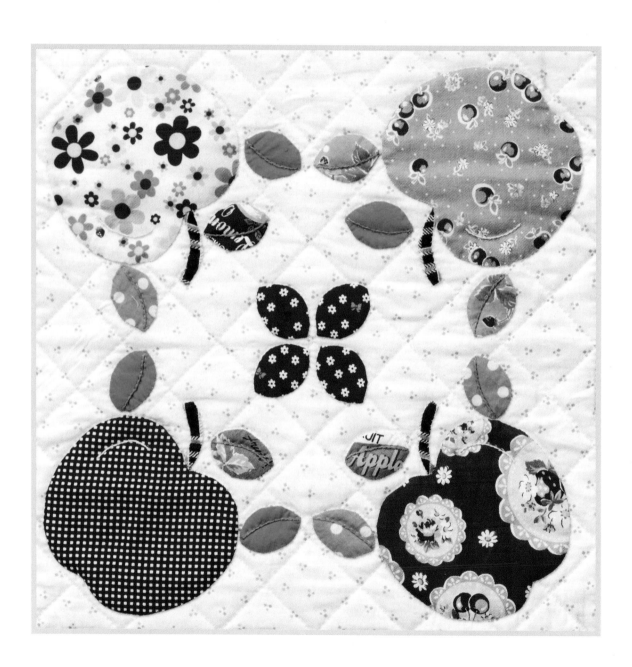

Cutting Instructions

Background fabric: (1) 13½" × 13½" square

A (4) from template   **C** (12) from template
B (4) from template   **D** (4) from template

Notes: Refer to photo on opposite page for appliqué orientation for the full block. Embroider the colored lines with stem stitch using 3 plies of floss (see page 67). Trim the finished block to 12½" × 12½".

FULL-SIZE TEMPLATE

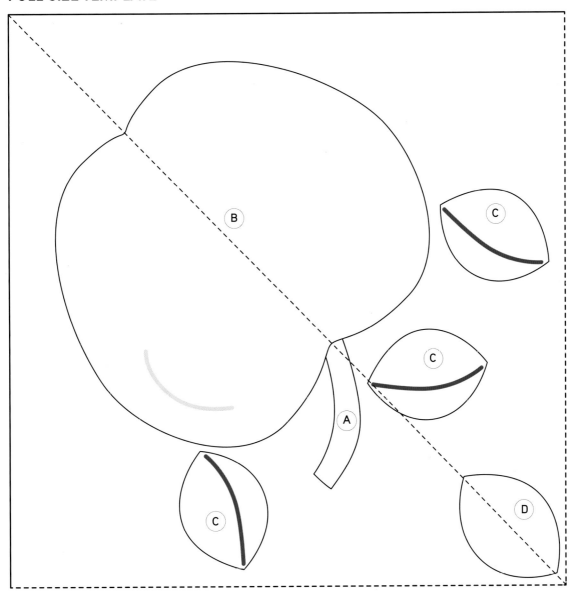

Cherries

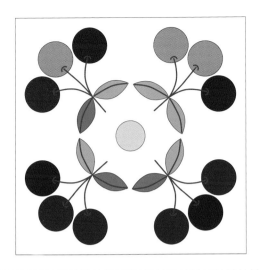

Cutting Instructions

Background fabric: (1) 13½" × 13½" square

A (12) from template   C (1) from template (use C
B (8) from template   from "Marguerite" block
                        on page 49)

Notes: Refer to photo on opposite page for appliqué
orientation for the full block. Embroider the colored lines
with stem stitch using 3 plies of floss (see page 67). Trim
the finished block to 12½" × 12½".

FULL-SIZE TEMPLATE

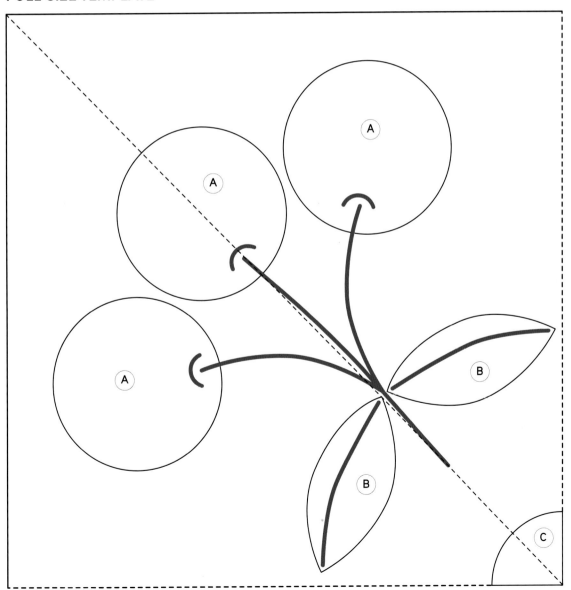

Strawberries

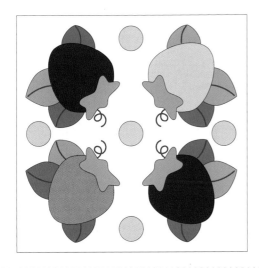

Cutting Instructions

Background fabric: (1) 13½" × 13½" square

A (4) from template   D (4) from template

B (4) from template   E (4) from template

C (4) from template   F (5) from template

Notes: Refer to photo on opposite page for appliqué orientation for the full block. Embroider the colored lines with stem stitch using 3 plies of floss (see page 67). Trim the finished block to 12½" × 12½".

FULL-SIZE TEMPLATE

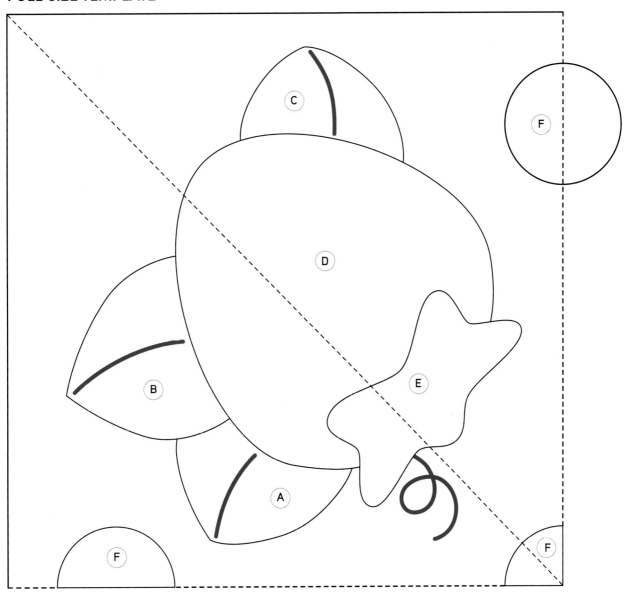

Pears

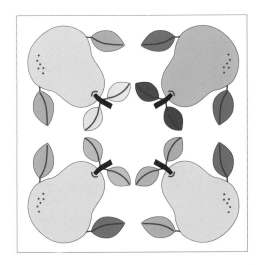

Cutting Instructions

Background fabric: (1) 13½" × 13½" square

A (4) from template   **C** (8) from template

B (4) from template   **D** (8) from template

Notes: Refer to photo on opposite page for appliqué orientation for the full block. Embroider the colored lines with stem stitch using 3 plies of floss (see page 67). Trim the finished block to 12½" × 12½".

FULL-SIZE TEMPLATE

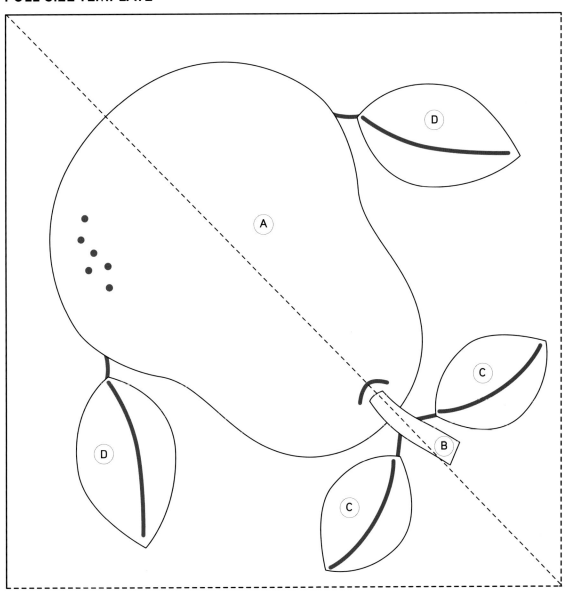

APPLIQUÉ TECHNIQUES

Appliqué may seem intimidating, but with a little practice, you can achieve beautiful results. Use the following techniques to create stunning needle-turn appliqué designs.

Templates

Align the background fabric on the template. Trace the block design onto the right side of the fabric with a non-permanent marker like chalk or a pencil. A light box may be helpful.

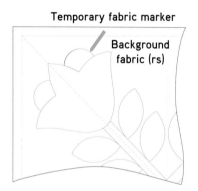

Temporary fabric marker

Background fabric (rs)

Trace an appliqué shape onto the non-shiny side of freezer paper. Cut out the shape along the traced lines.

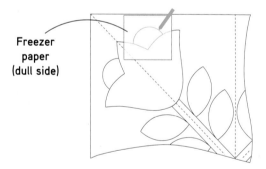

Freezer paper (dull side)

Cut a piece of fabric for the appliqué shape at least ½" larger than the template. Adhere the shiny side of the freezer paper shape to the right side of the fabric. Trim the fabric leaving ¼" seam allowance.

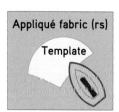

Appliqué fabric (rs)

Template

¼" seam allowance

Apply a bit of fabric glue to the wrong side of the appliqué shape. Adhere it to the background fabric as marked.

Fabric glue

(ws)

Using the paper template as a guide, use the needle to tuck the seam allowance underneath the fabric shape (called needle-turn appliqué). Hand stitch the appliqué shape using small stitches. Remove the paper.

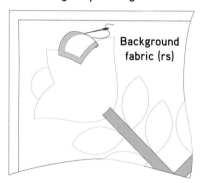

Needle-turn along template edge

Background fabric (rs)

Overlapping Shapes

When appliqué shapes overlap, add the bottom shape first. For edges of the bottom shape that will be covered by another shape, baste the edge(s) in place rather than needle-turning to reduce bulk.

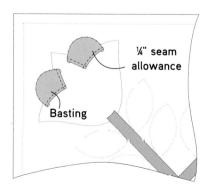

¼" seam allowance

Basting

Stems

Cut bias fabric strips and fusible web tape to the required width and length. Feed a few inches of both the fabric and fusible web tape strips through a bias tape maker. Use a pin to secure the fabric and fusible web ends to an ironing board. Fuse them together with an iron.

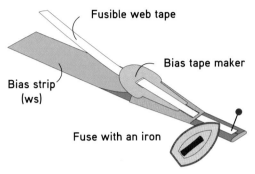

Remove the paper from the fusible web strip to expose the adhesive.

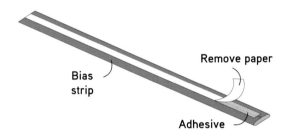

Position and fuse the bias strip, right side up, onto the traced background fabric. Appliqué stitch the stems in place.

For blocks with stems, always add the stems first. Note that straight stems do not need to be bias cut.

Corners and Points

Make a small clip into the seam allowance of inside corners and sharp points.

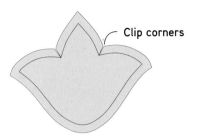

Fold seam allowance under with a needle to form a point.

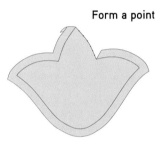

Make two or three overlapping stitches to secure these delicate areas in place.

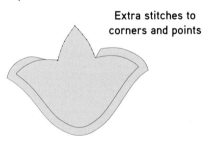

Embroidery

Use 3 plies of floss for all embroidery, unless otherwise noted.

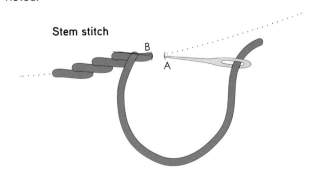

THE
Quilt & Projects

The *Vintage Flower* Sampler Quilt

This stunning sampler quilt is sure to become a family heirloom enjoyed by generations to come. Featuring 12 patchwork and 12 appliqué blocks, this quilt is perfect for using up your scrap stash! Each block measures 12" square and the finished quilt is twin sized.

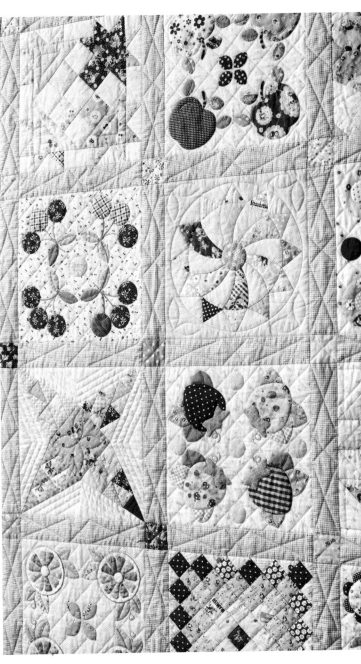

Requirements

- assorted fabric scraps
- 1¾ yards of sashing/border fabric
- 78" × 106" batting
- 6 ¼ yards backing fabric
- ½ yard binding fabric

Cutting Instructions

From the inner border/sashing fabric, cut:

- (2) 12½" × WOF strips. Cut into (32) 12½" × 2½" sashing strips.
- (2) 2½" × WOF strips. Cut into (6) 2½" × 12½" sashing strips.
- (7) 3½" × WOF strips. Piece for length and cut into (2) 3½" × 82½" inner side borders and (2) 3½" × 60½" inner top/bottom borders.

From assorted fabric scraps, cut:

- (327) 2½" squares

From binding fabric, cut:

- (8) 2" x WOF strips (or desired width)

1 Join the 24 blocks with the 38 sashing strips and 15 scrap squares as shown.

2 Add the inner side borders, then the inner top and bottom borders.

3 Join 88 squares into a side border panel of 2 squares by 44 squares. Make 2.

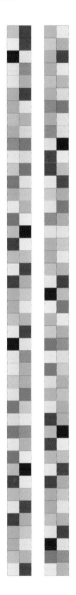

4 Join 68 squares into a side border panel of 2 squares by 34 squares. Make 2.

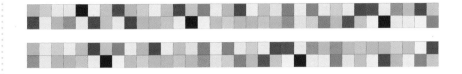

5 Add the side pieced borders first, then the top and bottom pieced borders.

FINISH THE QUILT

Once you've sewn your blocks together, it's time to assemble your quilt! Use the following guide to add the batting and backing, quilt your sampler, and bind the quilt.

Mark the Design

If you are planning an elaborate topstitch design, which is anything more than straight lines or random free-motion quilting, you need to draw your design on the quilt top before layering it with the batting and backing.

Be sure to use a marking tool that you can see on your fabrics. Test the marker on scrap fabrics first to ensure they can be removed.

Make a "Quilt Sandwich"

Layering a quilt top with batting and backing is commonly referred to as a quilt sandwich.

Each layer needs to be prepared:
• press and mark (see above) the quilt top.
• cut the batting 8" to 12" larger than the quilt top; press
• make the backing the same size as the batting

Depending on the width of the fabric, you may need to seam the backing:

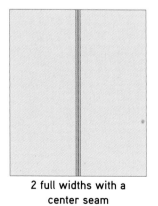

2 full widths with a
center seam

Lay the backing, wrong side up, on a flat surface, like a wood floor. Secure the edges with masking tape. The fabric should be pulled smooth, but if the edges form scallops between the pieces of tape, it is too tight.

Lay the batting onto the backing. Smooth out any folds or wrinkles.

Center the pressed and marked quilt top onto the batting. Smooth it out, ensuring the edges align with the backing.

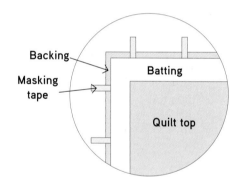

Starting at the center, pin or thread baste. Work diagonally to each corner. Pins or basting stitches should be 6" to 8" apart.

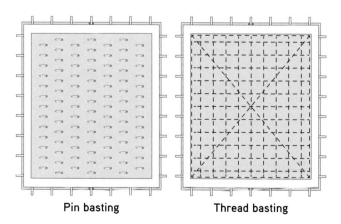

Pin basting   Thread basting

Quilt

Once your quilt sandwich is prepared, you are ready to quilt, either by hand or machine. The Vintage Flower Sampler Quilt was quilted by hand. Hand quilting is very popular in Japan. If you are new to hand quilting, it may seem difficult at first, but the more you practice, the more comfortable you will become and your skills will improve.

The beauty of samplers is that they allow you to play with different quilting designs. If you look closely at the photos of the quilt throughout the book, you'll notice that no two blocks are quilted exactly the same. Assorted quilting designs were used, including stitch in the ditch, grids, lines, and shapes.

When quilting a sampler, consider the individual block when determining the design. Use the lines of the block as a guide, then add more stitches to fill any open areas. If you're searching for quilting inspiration, refer to the individual block photos for ideas.

This close up photo of the quilting on the Lost Children block from page 28 shows three different types of quilting: diagonal lines, stitch in the ditch, and curves.

Double-Fold Binding

When your quilt is quilted, it is ready for binding. Although there are a few different ways to finish the edges of a quilt, double-fold binding is a very popular method among quilters.

Piece strips together with a mitered seam. Trim seam allowance to ¼". Press seam open.

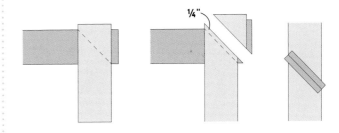

Fold the strip in half lengthwise, wrong sides together, and press. Lay binding along one quilt edge right sides together, aligning raw edges. Leaving a 6" tail, sew with ¼" seam allowance. Stop ¼" from the edge, sew a few reverse stitches.

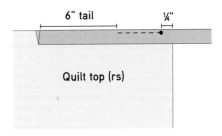

Fold the strip away from the quilt.

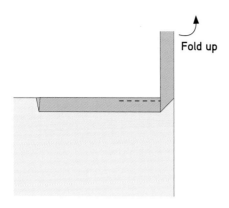

Fold it down along the next edge, aligning the raw edges. Sew from top edge down the quilt. Repeat at each corner.

Stop sewing 6" from where the seam starts. Overlap the end by the cut width of your binding. Trim the excess length.

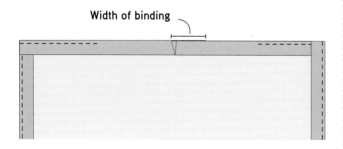

Open the fold at both ends. Align the ends as shown, right sides together. Pin and sew them together.

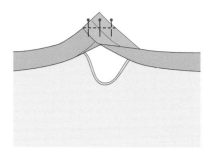

Trim the excess leaving a ¼" seam allowance.

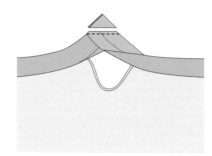

Press seam open and refold/press binding. Then finish sewing the binding to the quilt.

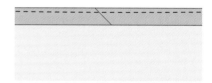

Fold binding over the raw quilt edges onto the back. Hand stitch the folded binding edge to the quilt back with an invisible stitch.

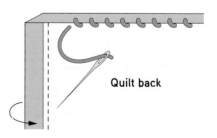

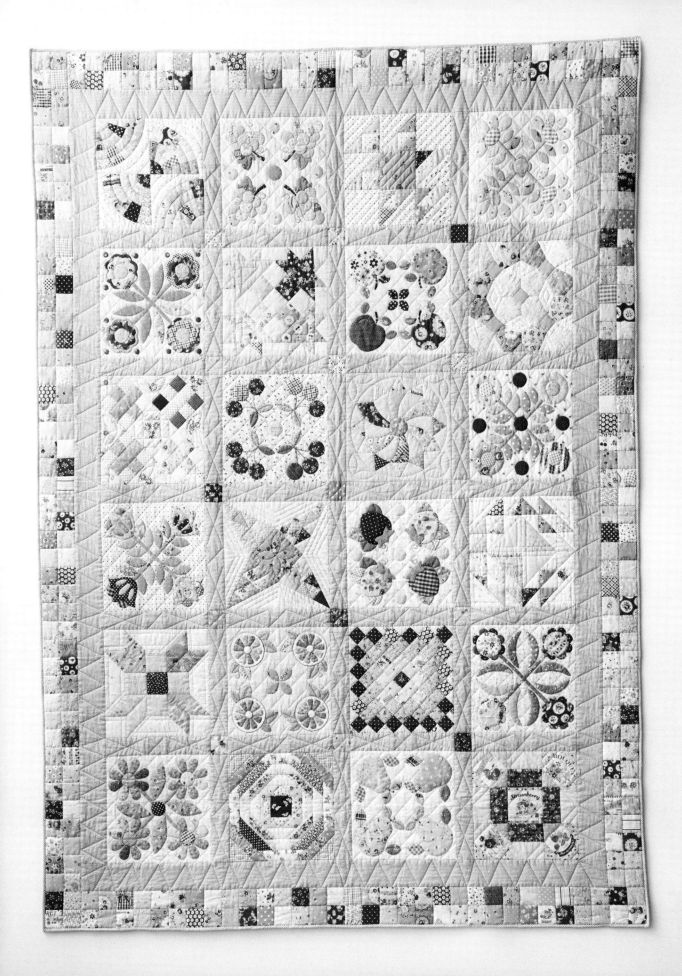

Vintage Vines Pillow

Leafy appliquéd vines make the perfect frame for your favorite patchwork or appliqué block. Try the Daisy block on page 46 or switch it out for another design. The pillow case features an easy envelope-style opening along the back and was made with a cheater print for maximum scrappiness.

Finished size: 17" × 17"

Requirements

- assorted scraps for appliqué
- 1 FQ background fabric
- ¼ yard border fabric
- 1 FQ appliqué lining fabric
- ½ yard backing fabric
- 20" × 20" batting
- 18" pillow form

Cutting Instructions

From background fabric, cut:

- (1) 13½" background square

From green FQ, cut:

- (2) ⅞" × 8¼" strips A
- 1" x 70" bias strip (pieced for length)

From assorted scraps, cut:

- (20) from template B
- (4) from template C
- (48) from template D
- (4) from template E
- (1) from template F (use C from "Marguerite" block on page 49)
- (24) from template G
- (4) from template H

From border fabric, cut:

- (2) 3½" × 12½" borders
- (2) 3½" × 18½" borders

From appliqué lining fabric, cut:

- (1) 18" background square

From backing fabric, cut:

- (2) 17½" × 14" rectangles

- See pages 47 and 116 for templates.
- Cutting dimensions include seam allowance.
- Sew using ¼" seam allowance.

1 Make a **Daisy** block (instructions on page 47). Add the borders.

18½" × 18½"

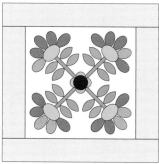

2 Refer to the instructions on page 67 to prepare the bias strip stems for appliqué.

3 Trace the inside line of the vine from the template onto the right side of the block border.

4 Fold one end of the vine to the wrong side by a ¼" and press. Pin that end onto the traced line and sew it in place. Continue stitching the vine to the border along the traced line.

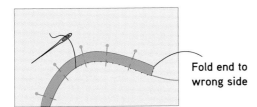

Fold end to wrong side

5 When the ends of the vine meet, fold the second end under and butt it neatly against the first folded end.

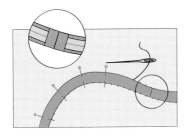

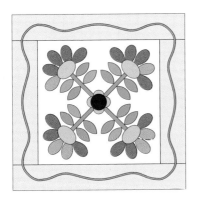

6 Complete the appliqué (templates on page 116).

7 Make a "quilt sandwich" (see page 74). Quilt as desired. Trim to 17½" square if necessary.

8 To make the pillow back, fold and press one long edge of a backing rectangle ½" twice to the wrong side to form a hem. Stitch the hem in place. Make 2 hemmed rectangles.

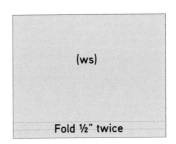

(ws)

Fold ½" twice

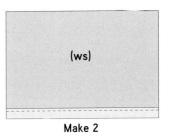

(ws)

Make 2

9 Lay a hemmed rectangle onto the appliqué, right sides together, aligning the top edges.

10 Repeat with the second hemmed rectangle, aligning the bottom edges.

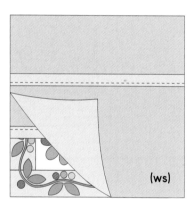

11 Pin and sew the layers together.

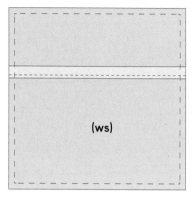

12 Turn the pillow right side out and insert the pillow form.

Farmer's Market Tote

Showcase your favorite block with this pretty and practical tote perfect for the farmer's market. The tote shown here features the Cross Plains block on page 20, and includes a side gusset providing generous storage.

Requirements

- assorted scraps for patchwork
- 1 FQ background fabric
- ½ yard body fabric
- ½ yard binding/handle fabric
- ½ yard lining fabric
- ½ yard fusible batting
- 1 yard rick rack, ⅜" wide

Cutting Instructions

From assorted scraps, cut:

- (4) 2⅝" squares A
- (4) 5⅜" squares, cut diagonally to make (8) B triangles (need 4)
- (16) 2" C squares

From background fabric, cut:

- (5) 2⅝" squares A
- (12) 2" × 3½" rectangles D
- (4) 2" squares E
- (2) 1¾" × 13" (handles) F

From body fabric, cut:

- (2) 2" × 12½" H
- (1) 40" × 6" (gusset)
- (1) 12½" × 15½" (back)

From binding/handle fabric, cut:

- (2) 2" × 46", bias cut (piece for length)
- (2) 2" × 13", bias cut
- (2) 2" × 3½", bias cut
- (2) 1¾" × 13" (handles) G

From lining fabric, cut:

- (2) 12½" × 15½"
- (1) 40" × 6" (gusset)

From fusible batting, cut:

- (2) 12½" × 15½"
- (2) 1¼" × 13" (handles)
- (1) 40" × 6" (gusset)

- Cutting dimensions include seam allowance.
- Sew using ¼" seam allowance.

---

1 Make a **Cross Plains** block (instructions on page 21). Add 2 [H] to make the bag front.

12½" × 15½"

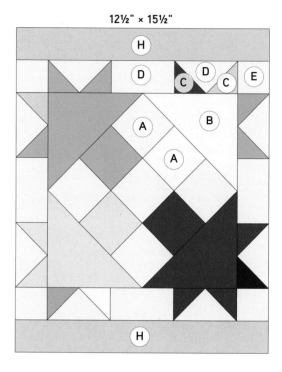

2 Make a "quilt sandwich," (see page 74), ensuring that the batting is adhered to the patchwork. Quilt as desired, and trim to 12½" × 15½".

3 Make a "quilt sandwich," ensuring that the batting is adhered to the bag back. Quilt as desired, and trim to 12½" × 15½".

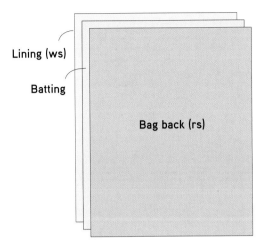

Lining (ws)

Batting

Bag back (rs)

4 To make a handle, sew [F] and [G], right sides together, down both long sides.

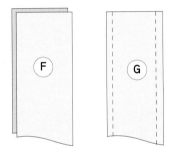

F

G

5 Fold the handle so the seams are in the middle as shown. Press seams open. Adhere the batting strip as shown.

Batting

6 Turn the handle right side out. Align the seams in the middle as shown, and press. Topstitch both edges with a ⅛" seam. Stitch the rickrack trim to cover the seam on one side only as shown. Make 2.

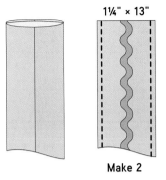

1¼" × 13"

Make 2

7 Lay a handle, rickrack side up, on the wrong side of the bag front, aligning the raw edges. Pin the handle ends 4" apart, and baste them in place with a scant ¼" seam.

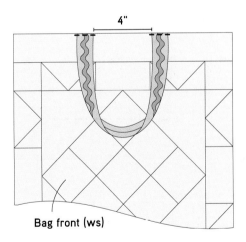

4"

Bag front (ws)

8 Bind the top edge of the bag front with a 2" × 13" bias strip. Trim if necessary.

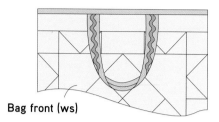

Bag front (ws)

9 Fold the handle up. Hand stitch the handle to the top edge of the binding as shown. Add a handle to the bag back.

10 To make the gusset, make a "quilt sandwich," ensuring that the batting is adhered to the gusset. Quilt as desired and trim to 38½" x 4½".

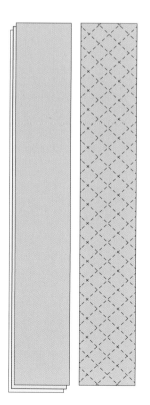

11 Fold the quilted gusset strip in half crosswise. Mark 6" up from the fold on both sides. Mark ¾" over from the outside edge on the top ends. Align a ruler with the marks along one side and trim as shown. Trim the other side.

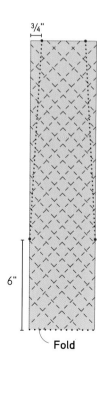

¾"

6"

Fold

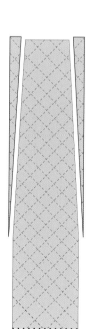

12 Bind both ends with a 2" × 3" bias strip (refer to page 75) for binding instructions). Trim if necessary.

13 Mark the center points of the gusset and the bottom bag front with pins. With wrong sides together, align the pins. Pin and sew the gusset to the bag front as shown, slightly rounding the corners. Note that the gusset will start 1" below the top edge of the bag. Trim the bottom corners. Repeat to add the bag back.

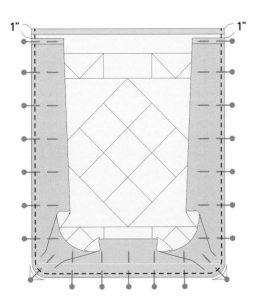

14 Bind the seam allowances.

Scrappy **Table Runner**

Dress up your dining table or sideboard with a pretty patchwork table runner. The half-square triangle sashing complements the shape of the Cat's Cradle block from page 16.

Finished size: 48½" × 16½"

Requirements

- assorted red scraps
- assorted pink, blue, green, orange, and yellow scraps
- 1 yard background fabric
- 1¼ yards backing fabric
- ¼ yard binding fabric
- 20" × 52" batting

Cutting Instructions

From assorted red fabrics, cut:

- (3) 4½" A squares
- (16) 2⅞" squares, cut diagonally to make (32) B triangles

From assorted scraps, cut:

- (27) 2⅞" squares, cut diagonally to make (54) B triangles

From background fabric, cut:

- (6) 4½" A squares
- (25) 2⅞" squares cut diagonally to make (50) B triangles
- (9) 4⅞" squares cut diagonally to make (18) C triangles.
- (5) 2½" × WOF strips. Cut into (4) 2½" × 14½" D, and (2) 2½" × 12½" E.

From binding fabric, cut:

- (3) 2" × WOF strips, piece for length

Optional: Cut the **B** squares 3¼" and trim the HSTs to 2½".

- Cutting dimensions include seam allowance.
- Sew using ¼" seam allowance.

---

1 Make 3 **Cat's Cradle** blocks (instructions on page 17).

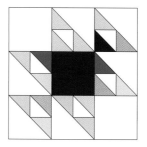

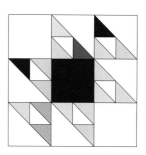

12½" × 12½"

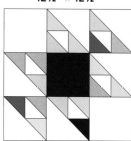

2 Join a red and a background [B] triangle to make a half-square triangle unit (HST). Make 32.

2½" × 2½"

Make 32

3 Join 6 HSTs to make a sashing strip. Make 4.

2½" × 12½"

Make 4

4 Join the blocks and sashing strips. Add 2 [E] strips to the ends.

48½" × 12½"

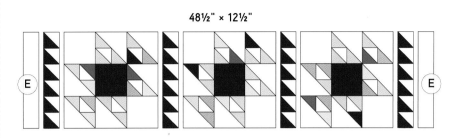

5 Join 4 HSTs, 2 [D] and [E] to make a border. Make 2.

48½" × 2½"

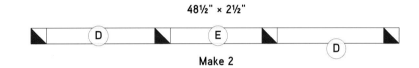

Make 2

6 Add the borders.

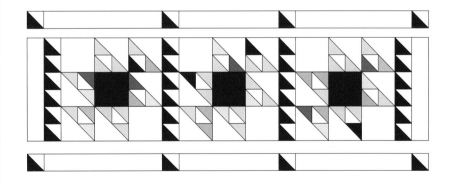

7 Make a "quilt sandwich" (see page 74). Quilt as desired, and bind.

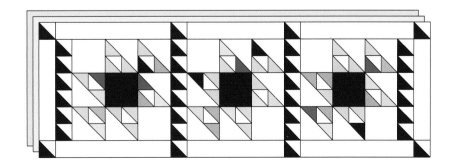

Drawstring Pouch

Keep your craft projects organized with this sweet drawstring pouch. It features the Sunflower appliqué block from page 44 framed by flying geese borders. Special details, such as the lace drawstring casing and covered buttons, add a finishing touch.

Requirements

- assorted scraps for patchwork and appliqué
- 1 FQ green fabric
- ⅓ yard background fabric
- ¼ yard contrast fabric
- 1 FQ lining fabric
- 12" × 30" fusible batting
- 72" of cording
- 21" length of 2" wide, double-edged, flat lace with holes to thread cording
- Four 1" diameter covered buttons (Item #ZW6370 at zakkaworkshop.com)

Cutting Instructions

From green FQ, cut:

- (1) ⅞" × 5" strips A
- (2) from template D

From assorted scraps, cut:

- (8) from template B
- (1) from template C
- (24) 1½" × 2½" F
- (4) 3½" squares

From background fabric, cut:

- (1) 7½" square G
- (48) 1½" squares H

From contrast fabric, cut:

- (2) 10½" × 6½" I
- (1) 10½" × 3½" J

From lining fabric, cut:

- (1) 10½" × 27½"

- See pages 45 and 117 for templates.
- Cutting dimensions include seam allowance.
- Sew using ¼" seam allowance.

---

1 Make one quarter of the **Sunflower** block (instructions on page 45). Trim to 6½" square.

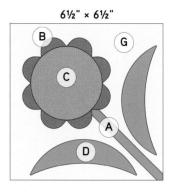

6½" × 6½"

2 Using Sew and Flip (see page 38), add 2 [H] to [F] to make a flying geese unit. Make 24.

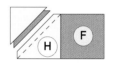 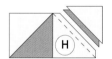

2½" × 1½"

Make 24

3 Join 6 geese to make a 2½" × 6½" strip. Make 4.

2½" × 6½"

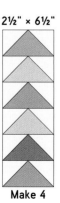

Make 4

4 Add 2 geese strips to the Sunflower block.

10½" × 6½"

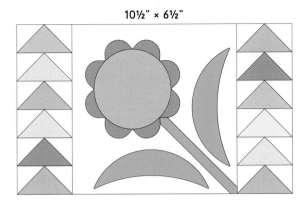

5 Sew the four 3½" squares together. Add 2 geese strips.

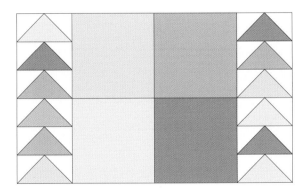

6 Join the assembled blocks, 2 [I], and [J] as shown.

10½" × 27½"

7 Adhere the batting to the wrong side of the body, and quilt as desired.

8 With right sides together, fold in half and sew the side seams. Press seams open. Cut 1" squares from the bottom corners.

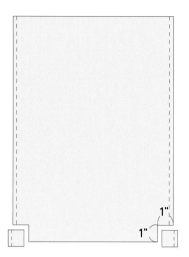

9 Fold the body to align the side seam with the bottom center. Sew across the notch to form the bottom corner. Repeat with the other notch.

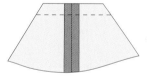

10 Turn the bag right side out.

11 Repeat steps 8-9 to form the bag lining, leaving a 4" opening along one side seam.

12 With right sides together, insert the bag into the lining. Align the top edges and side seams. Pin and sew around the top.

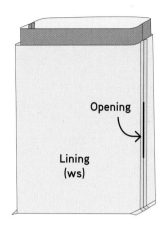
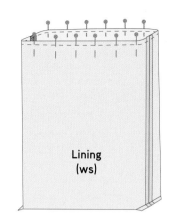

13 Turn the bag right side out through the lining opening. Stitch the opening closed and fit the lining inside the bag. Press the top edge seam.

14 Cut the lace into two 10" lengths. Fold the raw ends of one lace length twice by ¼" to form a hem. Position the length 1½" down from the top edge and about ⅛" away from the side seam. Pin and hand sew in place. Repeat to add the second lace length.

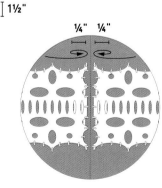

15 Cut two 36" lengths of cording. Fit a small safety pin to the end of one cord, and thread it through the lace, starting and stopping at the same side seam.

16 Repeat with the other cord, starting and stopping at the opposite side seam.

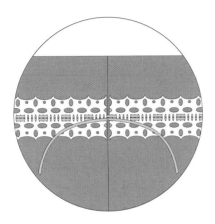

17 Sew a running stitch by hand near the edge of [E], and place a button dome on the wrong side of the circle. Pull the thread until the fabric is gathered snuggly around the dome, and secure the gathered stitches with a knot. Make 4.

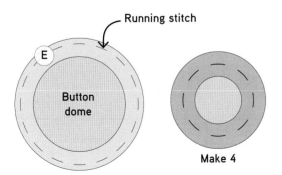

Running stitch

E

Button dome

Make 4

18 Lay the ends of one cord together on the wrong side of a covered button. Stitch or glue them in place. Lay a second covered button against the first one, wrong sides together, and join them around the edges with a ladder stitch. Repeat with the other cord ends.

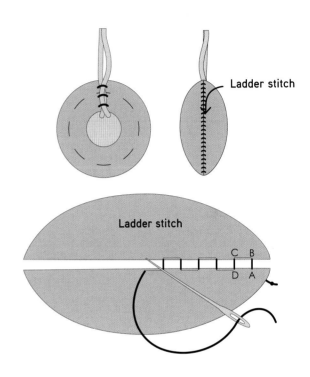

Ladder stitch

Ladder stitch

Patchwork **Purse**

Use any of the appliqué motifs to embellish this sweet little coin purse. It's the ideal size for one flower or piece of fruit...or skip the appliqué entirely and let the patchwork design shine!

Finished size: 6½" × 8" × 3"

Requirements

- assorted scraps for appliqué
- assorted scraps for background
- 1 FQ gusset fabric
- 1 FQ appliqué lining fabric
- 1 FQ lightweight fusible batting
- Green and white embroidery floss
- 7" × 3½" rose gold purse clasp
  (Item #ZW6356 at zakkworkshop.com)
- Tools for installing clasp: Craft glue, toothpicks, stiletto or flat-head screwdriver, pliers

Cutting Instructions

From stem scrap, cut:
- (1) from template A

From apple scrap, cut:
- (1) from template B

From leaf scraps, cut:
- (3) from template C

From background scraps, cut:
- (2) 4½" square D
- (2) 4½" × 2" E
- (2) 6" × 3½" F
- (2) 3½" × 7½" G

From gusset fabric, cut:
- (1) from gusset template

From lining fabric, cut:
- (2) from body template
- (1) from gusset template

From fusible batting, cut:
- (2) from body template (no seam allowance)
- (1) from gusset template (no seam allowance)

- See pages 59 and 118-119 for templates.
- Cutting dimensions include seam allowance.
- Sew using ¼" seam allowance.

1. Join [D] and [E]. Add [F], and then [G] as shown below. Make 2 (front and back panels).

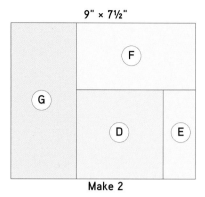

9" × 7½"

Make 2

2. Appliqué an apple from the **Apples** block (instructions on page 59) onto the front panel.

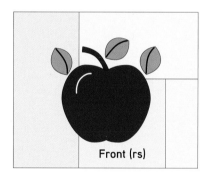

Front (rs)

3. Embroider the apple highlight and leaf veins with stem stitch using 3 plies of floss.

4. Adhere the batting to the wrong side of both panels, and quilt as desired.

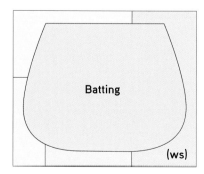

Batting

(ws)

5 Use the body template to cut out both panels. Use a fabric pen to mark the alignment dots from the template onto the wrong side of both body pieces.

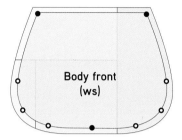

Body front (ws)

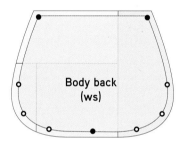

Body back (ws)

6 Adhere the batting to the wrong side of the gusset, and quilt as desired. Use a fabric pen to mark the alignment dots from the template onto the wrong side of the gusset.

7 Align the bottom center of the body front with the center of the gusset as shown, right sides together. Pin.

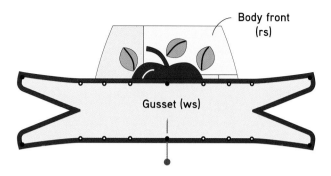

Body front (rs)

Gusset (ws)

8 Pin the rest of the gusset to a body piece, aligning all the dots. Sew the pieces together. Clip the curves and press the seam open. Repeat to add the other body piece.

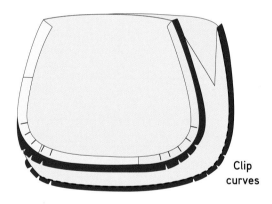

Clip curves

9 Make the lining the same way as the body.

10 Insert the lining into the body with right sides together. Pin and sew around the top edges. Pivot at the "V" on the gusset, and leave a 3" opening along the body back.

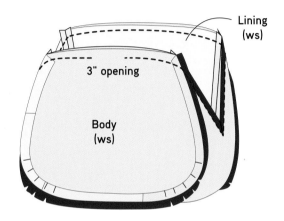

11 Turn right side out and press.

12 Pin and sew around the opening with a ⅛" seam.

13 Cut the paper string into pieces matching the length of the top and sides of the purse clasp.

14 Use a toothpick to apply craft glue to the inside groove of one half of the clasp.

15 Insert the top edge of the purse front into the glued half of the clasp, making sure the center of the purse is aligned with the center of the clasp. Then insert the sides (gusset edges) into the groove.

16 Use a stiletto or flat-head screwdriver to insert the pieces of paper string into the groove on the inside of the clasp.

17 Wrap the clasp with a piece of batting to protect the metal, and then gently squeeze with a pair of pliers to "pinch" the fabric within the groove. Caution: Squeezing the metal too hard will cause dents, so be gentle and go slow.

18 Let the glue dry for 15 minutes, and then repeat this process with the other half of the clasp.

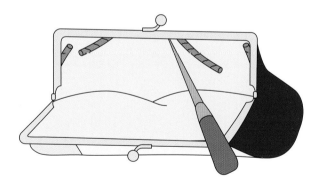

PATCHWORK TEMPLATES

Pineapple
Page 22

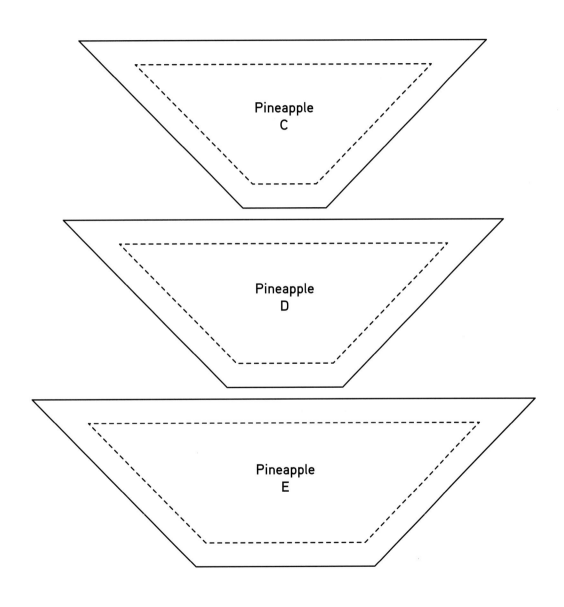

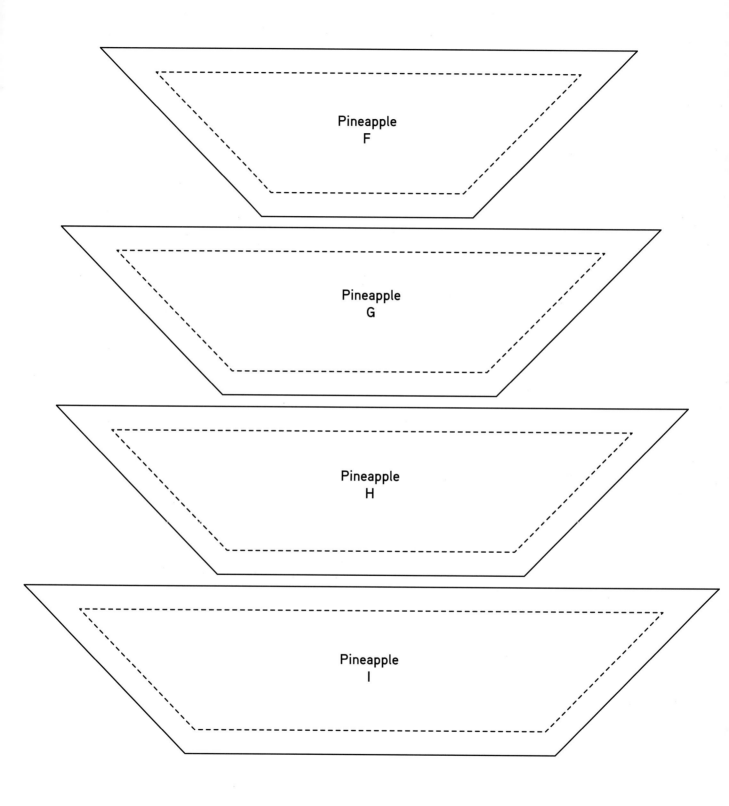

Pineapple
F

Pineapple
G

Pineapple
H

Pineapple
I

Parisienne
Page 26

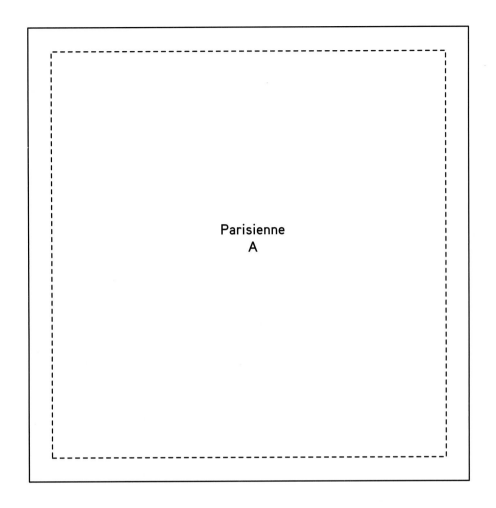

Parisienne
A

Parisienne
B

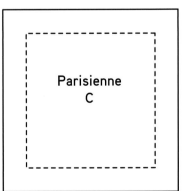

Parisienne
C

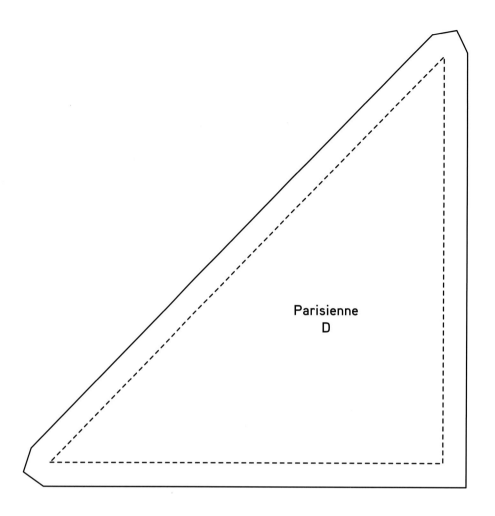

Parisienne
D

Around the World
Page 24

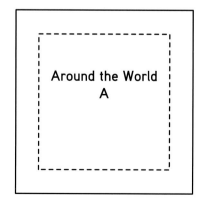

Around the World
A

Lost Children
Page 28

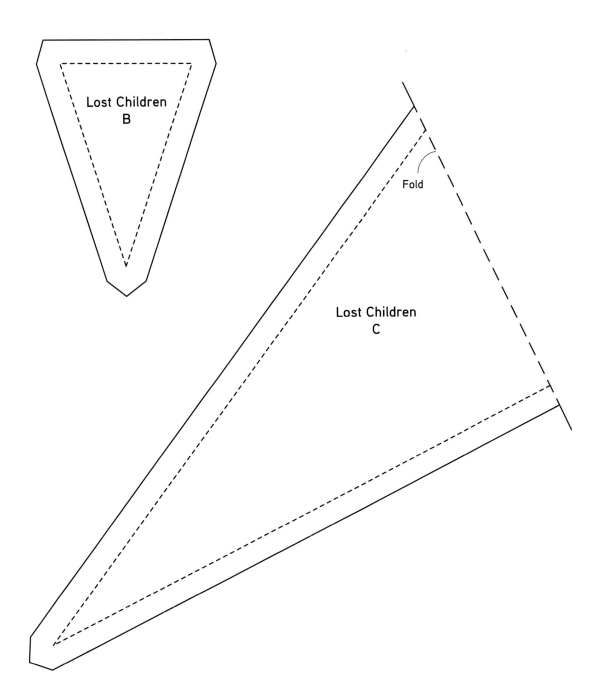

Lost Children
B

Lost Children
C

Fold

Farmer's Daughter

Page 30

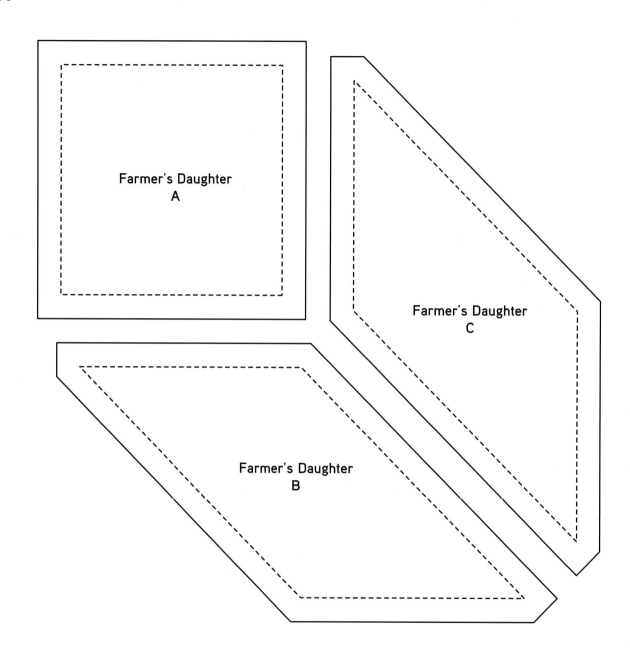

Farmer's Daughter
A

Farmer's Daughter
C

Farmer's Daughter
B

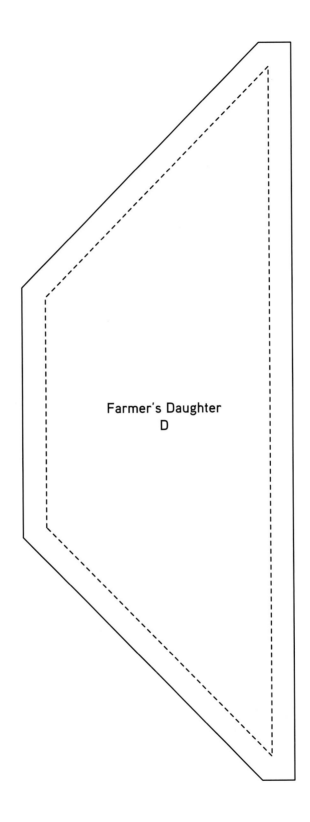

Farmer's Daughter
D

Tallahassee
Page 32

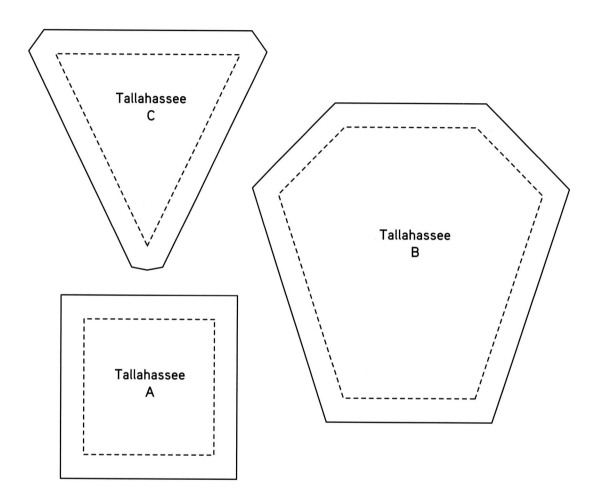

Lattice Fan

Page 34

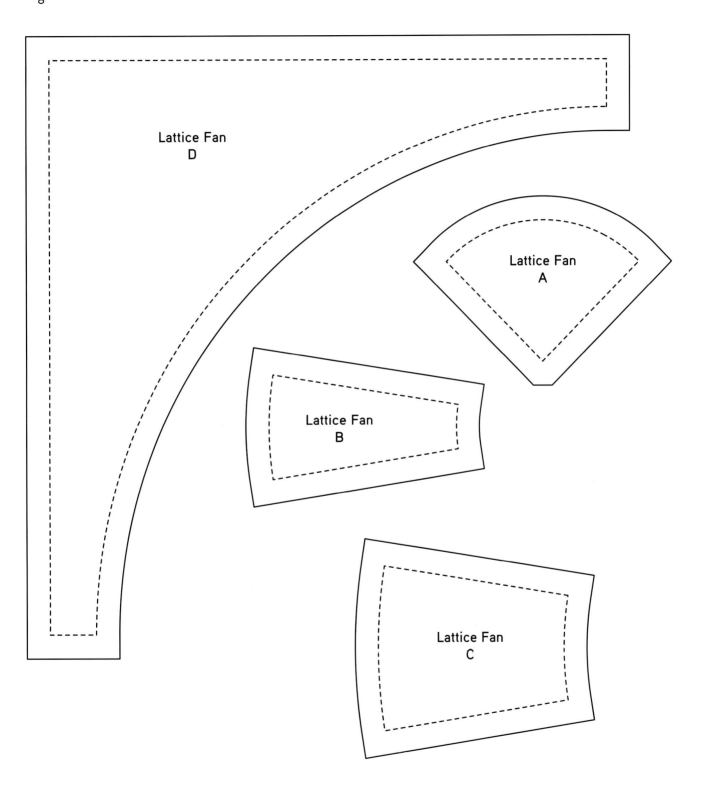

Lattice Fan
D

Lattice Fan
A

Lattice Fan
B

Lattice Fan
C

Sugar Plum
Page 36

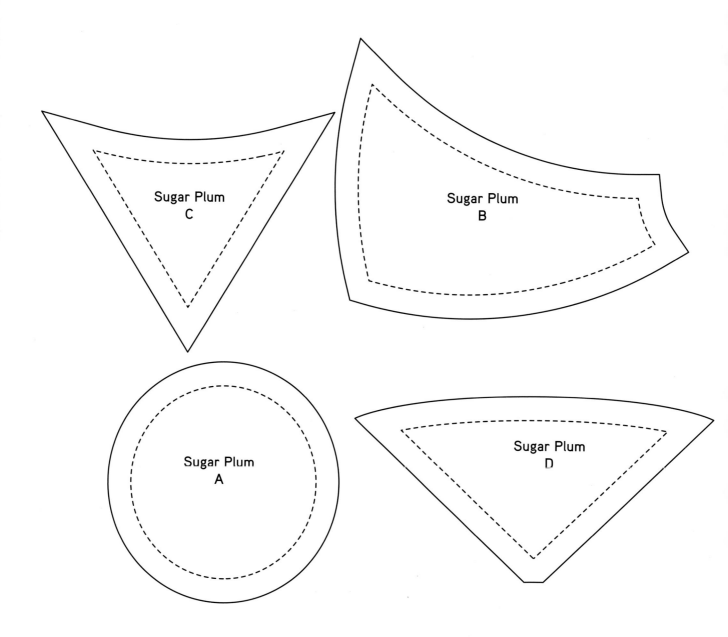

Sugar Plum
C

Sugar Plum
B

Sugar Plum
A

Sugar Plum
D

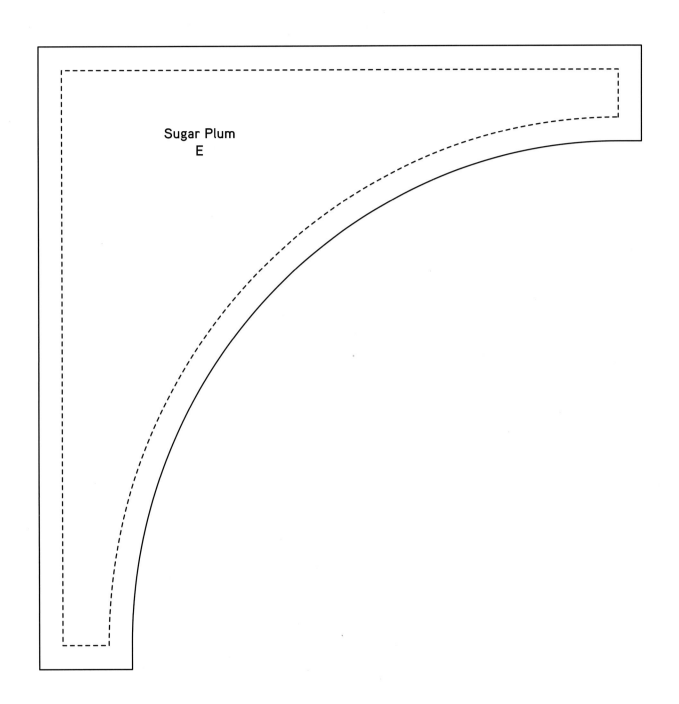

Sugar Plum
E

PROJECT TEMPLATES

Vintage Vines Pillow
Page 80

Side Border

Top/Bottom Border

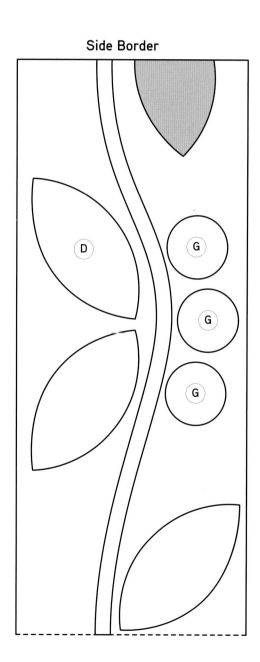

Border Design for Vintage Vines Pillow

Top/Bottom Border

Side Border

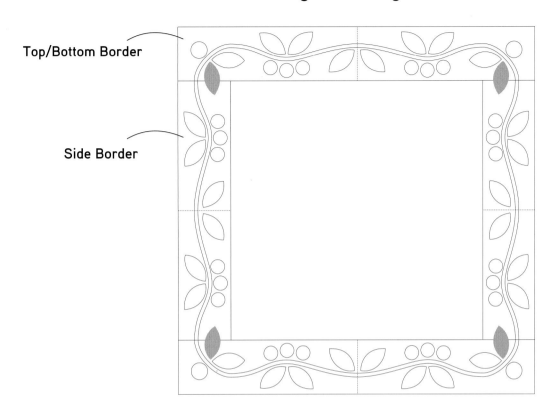

Drawstring Pouch
Page 96

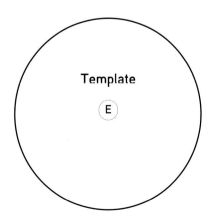

Template

E

Patchwork Purse
Page 102

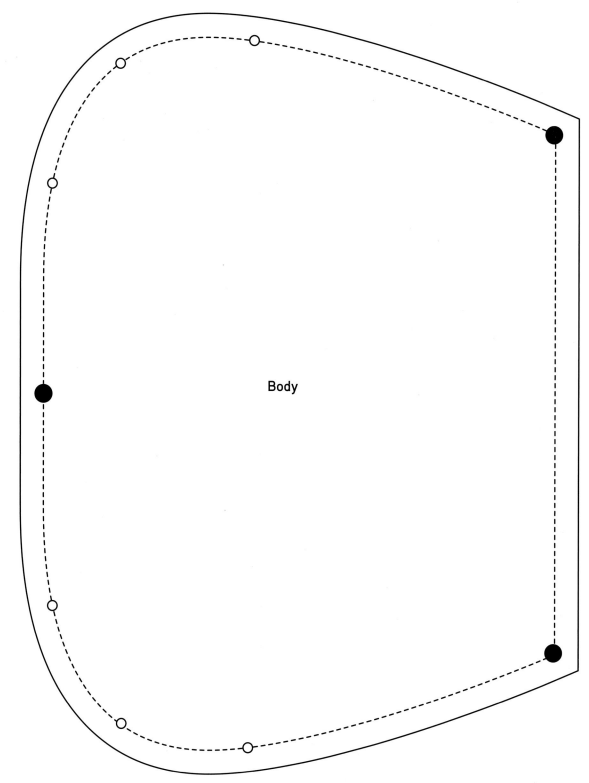

Body

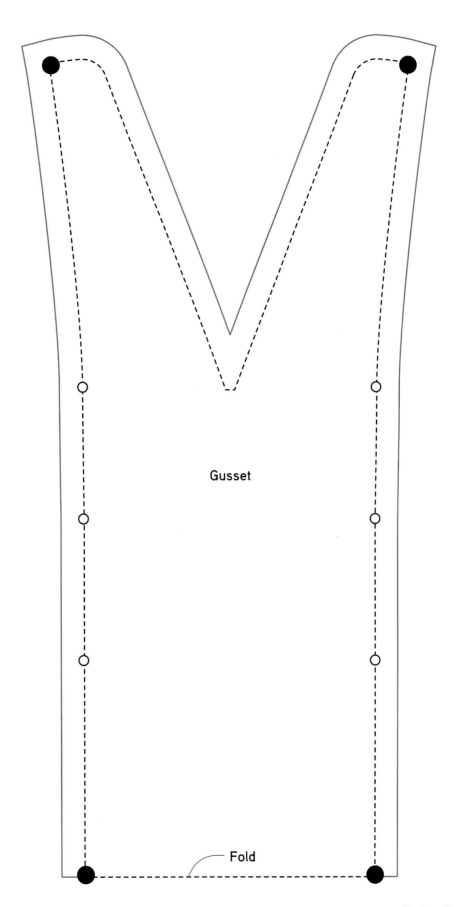

Gusset

Fold

RESOURCES

USA

Etsy
www.etsy.com
Great source for Atsuko Matsuyama fabric, as well as vintage feedsacks.
Ships from sellers based around the world.

Sunny Day Supply
www.sunnydaysupply.com
Online shop with an extensive assortment of Atsuko Matsuyama fabric.
Ships from the United States.

Zakka Workshop
www.zakkaworkshop.com
Source for metal purse frames, covered buttons, and other bag hardware.
Ships from the United States.

UK

Rose Garden Patchwork
www.rosegardenpatchwork.co.uk
Online shop with a wide assortment of Atsuko Matsuyama fabric. Ships
from the United Kingdom.

The Homemakery
www.thehomemakery.co.uk
Offers a wide assortment of 1930s reproduction fabric. Ships from the
United Kingdom.

JAPAN

A-Two Quilt Studio
www.a-two.com
Atsuko Matsuyama's quilt shop featuring her favorite fabric, notions, and
tools. Shipping within Japan only.

Yuwa Fabrics
www.yuwafabrics.e-biss.jp
Manufacturer of Atsuko Matsuyama fabric.